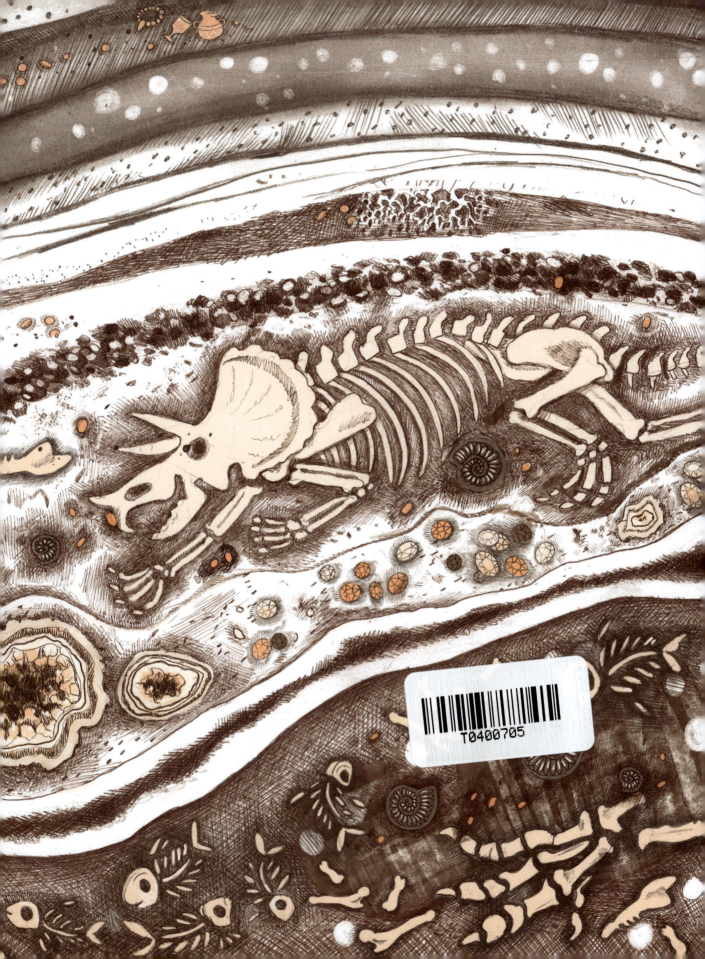

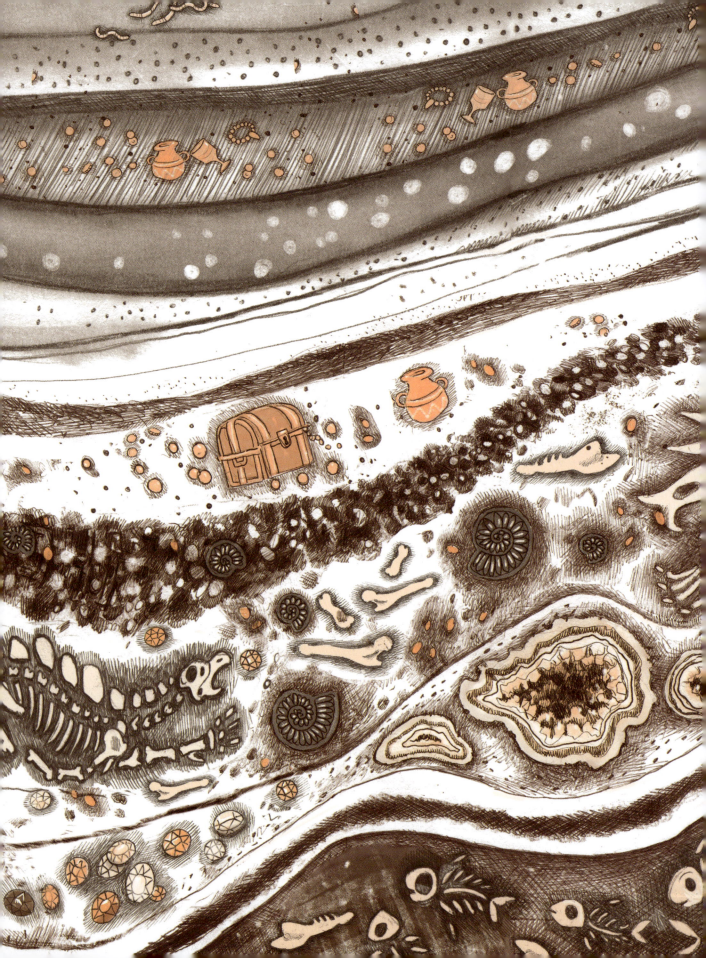

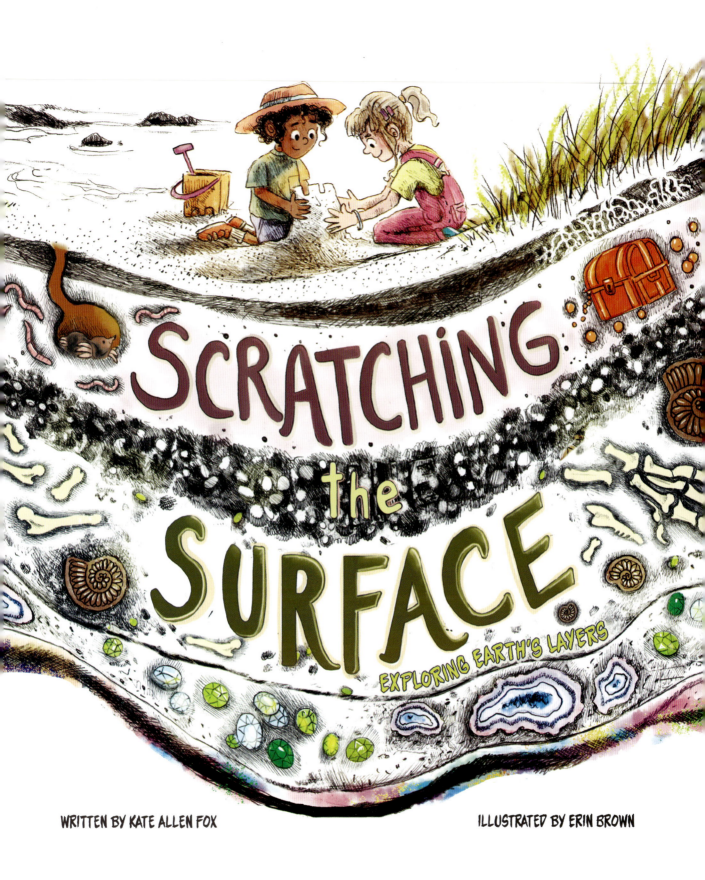

Published by Capstone Editions,
an imprint of Capstone
1710 Roe Crest Drive,
North Mankato, Minnesota 56003
capstonepub.com

Text copyright © 2025 by Kate Allen Fox
Illustrations copyright © 2025 by Erin Brown

All rights reserved. No part of this publication may be reproduced in whole or in part, or stored in a retrieval system, or transmitted in any form or by any means, electronic, mechanical, photocopying, recording, or otherwise, without written permission of the publisher.

Library of Congress Cataloging-in-Publication Data is available on the Library of Congress website.
ISBN: 9781630793326 (hardcover)
ISBN: 9781630793333 (ebook PDF)

Summary: A lyrical, scientific exploration of what's below our feet, this illustrated informational picture book digs into geological discoveries—and embraces the mysteries science has yet to solve. Join "science poet" Kate Allen Fox on a journey to the center of Earth in this wonder-filled investigation of Earth's layers.

Designed by Kay Fraser

Any additional websites and resources referenced in this book are not maintained, authorized, or sponsored by Capstone. All product and company names are trademarks™ or registered® trademarks of their respective holders.

The author gratefully acknowledges the assistance of Dr. Dayanthie Weeraratne, full professor of geology at California State University, Northridge.

For Pat and Mike —KAF

Far beneath forests and fields,
far beneath the waves,
in places no human has ever been,
lurk mysteries large and small.

What's beneath our feet?

What's inside our planet?

Why do volcanoes form and continents shift?

Our Earth, like any good mystery, contains layers of surprises, each uncovered in its own time.

Hidden inside our familiar planet are places
     unfamiliar and unforgiving,
     unseen and unsurvivable,
     unknown . . . but maybe not unknowable.

Let's explore.

CRUST

Earth's first layer, the crust, begins beneath our feet, where worms wriggle and writhe.

It's the only layer humans have sunk their shovels into.

Through its rocky terrain, we've dug mines and boreholes, but those only scratch the surface of our planet.

MOUNT EVEREST

the KOLA BOREHOLE

Though the crust makes up just 1 percent of Earth, we know more about it than any other layer. The deepest hole ever dug is the Kola Superdeep Borehole in Russia, which is 7.6 miles (12.2 kilometers) deep. That may not be so far *across* land, but 7.6 miles *down*? That's deep!

Over years and years, we've discovered more.
We learned what the crust is made of—
rocks called granite and basalt that are
rich in elements like oxygen, silicon,
and aluminum.

We learned how the temperature goes
up the farther *down* we go,
reaching up to 750 degrees Fahrenheit—
twice as hot as an oven baking cookies.

We kept digging deeper and deeper,
searching for answers,
until we could dig no farther.

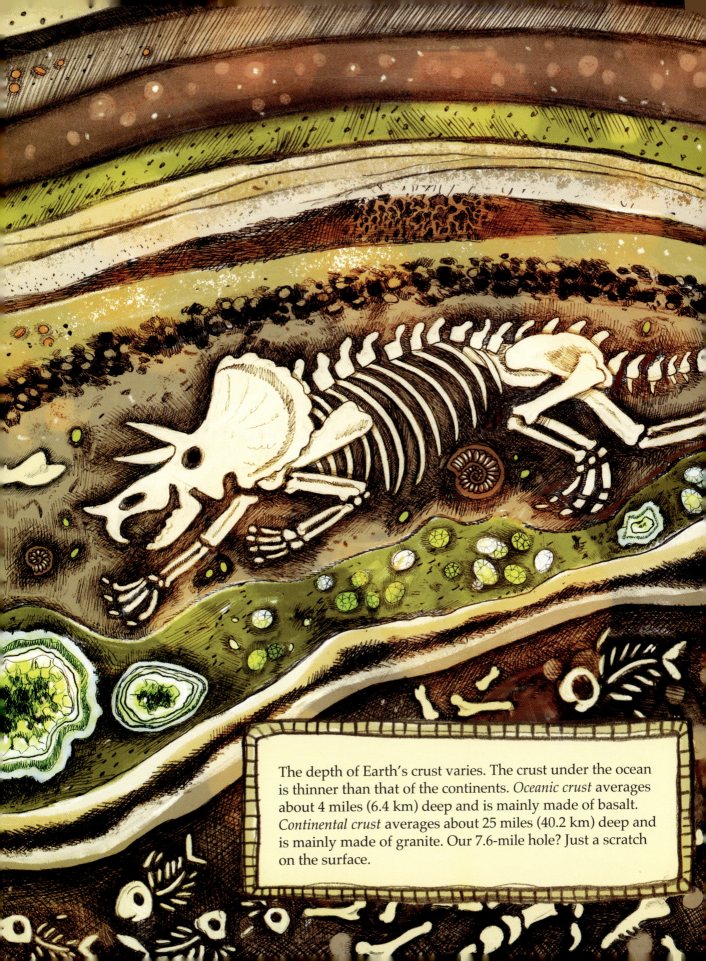

The depth of Earth's crust varies. The crust under the ocean is thinner than that of the continents. *Oceanic crust* averages about 4 miles (6.4 km) deep and is mainly made of basalt. *Continental crust* averages about 25 miles (40.2 km) deep and is mainly made of granite. Our 7.6-mile hole? Just a scratch on the surface.

MANTLE

Beneath the crust lies the mantle, where rock begins to become molten as heat and pressure build.

The massive mantle stretches down for 1,800 miles, making up nearly 85 percent of Earth's bulk.

No one has ever visited the mantle, but sometimes the magma that forms there visits us, blasting up through the crust and out of volcanoes, then cooling to create new land.

The mantle powers *plate tectonics*. Earth's continents sit on massive "plates" that float on top of the mantle. The mantle moves the plates, allowing continents to shift and mountains to form. Colliding plates can also cause earthquakes.

Another surprise the mantle has in store for us? Its harsh heat and intense pressure can transform an element called carbon into diamonds.

These jewels may one day rise **up** **up** **up** to the crust where we might find them.

Temperatures soar from a sizzling 1,832° F (1,000° Celsius) at the top of the mantle to a scorching 6,692° F (3,700° C) at the bottom. Pressure also becomes more and more extreme deeper in the mantle.

OUTER CORE

Beneath the mantle lurks the liquid outer core—swirling and shimmering with iron and nickel.

This mass of moving metal, buried thousands of miles below us, remains a mystery in many ways . . .

Unlike the crust and mantle, which are made of rock, the core is made of metal. Until recent decades, scientists thought that the core was only made of iron. Now they believe the outer core's iron is likely mixed with nickel and other nonmetallic elements.

There's so much heat and pressure in the core that even *if* machines could reach it, no tools could survive there— and certainly not people!

Upper Mantle

While scientists can't visit the core, they can still study it—and what it does—with invisible waves.

Lower mantle

Outer Core

Scientists use earthquake waves to learn about Earth's inner layers. By measuring how the waves move through the layers, they may be able to determine whether a layer is liquid or solid and what it's made of.

INNER CORE

Finally, almost 4,000 miles below where you sit,
at the center of our planet,
spins a solid sphere,
smaller than Earth's moon
and as hot as the surface of the sun—
the inner core—
the deepest,
hottest,
highest-pressure
place
on
Earth.

> Due to the intense pressure at the center of Earth, the inner core is solid metal rather than liquid like the outer core. The temperature of the inner core is estimated to reach *almost* 10,000° F (5,500° C)!

Together, the inner and outer cores do something extraordinary . . .

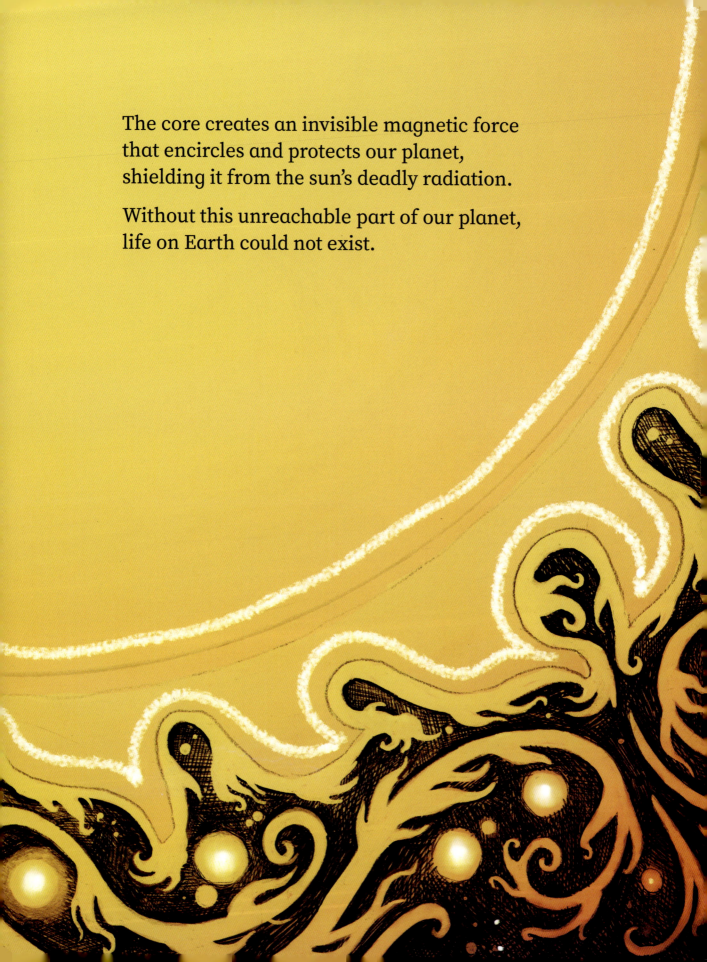

The core creates an invisible magnetic force that encircles and protects our planet, shielding it from the sun's deadly radiation.

Without this unreachable part of our planet, life on Earth could not exist.

But we do exist. And because we do, we can wonder and ponder and learn.

Scientists believe that Earth did not always have a magnetic field, but evidence suggests it has existed for at least 3 billion years. Electric currents moving through the iron in Earth's core generate a magnetic field. This field acts like a shield around Earth—deflecting solar particles and energy that would harm Earth's atmosphere and make life here impossible.

In the future, scientists will discover more about our planet.

Some of our ideas will be proven wrong.

But that's the great thing about science.

We learn

    and we guess

        and we try

            and we fail

                and we try again.

We hope to be right more often than we're wrong.

It's a lot like being human.

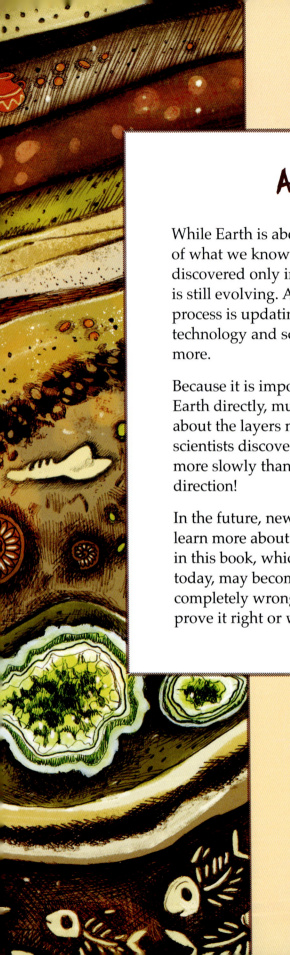

AUTHOR'S NOTE

While Earth is about 4.55 billion years old, much of what we know about Earth's layers has been discovered only in the past 100 years, and the science is still evolving. An important part of the scientific process is updating and changing what we know as technology and science advance and allow us to learn more.

Because it is impossible to study the inner layers of Earth directly, much of what scientists understand about the layers may change over time. Recently, scientists discovered that Earth's core is rotating more slowly than it used to—and may even reverse direction!

In the future, new technology may allow scientists to learn more about the layers. Some of the information in this book, which reflects science as we understand it today, may become outdated. Some of it may even be completely wrong! Maybe *you* can be the scientist to prove it right or wrong.

THE SCIENTIFIC METHOD

Scientific discovery is an *iterative* process—meaning that it will be repeated over time. There are five main steps to the scientific method:

1. **Ask a question**—Based on your observations of the world, ask a question.

2. **Make a hypothesis**—A hypothesis is your best guess at the answer to your question.

3. **Do an experiment**—Design an experiment to test your question.

4. **Gather data**—Collect the results of your experiment.

5. **Draw a conclusion**—Based on the evidence, do your best to answer your original question. Did the results of the experiment support your hypothesis, or did you learn something new?

Even after you've found your conclusion, you—or another scientist—can test the same question again to see if the results are the same. Or, you might ask a slightly different question on the same topic to add to your understanding. This is how scientists learn more and more about our world—by asking questions, double-checking their results, and finding new questions to ask.

GLOSSARY

continent—one of the six or seven land divisions on Earth

core—the innermost part of the planet—divided into inner and outer layers—which is made up of metal and creates Earth's magnetic field

crust—the outermost layer of the planet—divided into continental and oceanic types—which is made up of rock

element—a pure substance that cannot be broken down into something else

mantle—the second outermost layer of the planet, which is made up of semisolid rock and which powers plate tectonics

molten—a semiliquid state, which allows a substance to flow, especially at very high temperatures

plate tectonics—the movement of Earth's plates on top of the mantle; plate tectonics are responsible for the movement of continents, the formation of mountains, and earthquakes

radiation—energy moving from one place to another, often as waves

READ MORE

Cerullo, Mary M. *Volcano, Where Fire and Water Meet*. North Mankato, MN: Capstone, 2021.

Fox, Kate Allen. *Pando: A Living Wonder of Trees*. North Mankato, MN: Capstone, 2021.

Lukidis, Lydia. *Deep, Deep Down: The Secret Underwater Poetry of the Mariana Trench*. North Mankato, MN: Capstone, 2023.

Lukidis, Lydia. *Up, Up High: The Secret Poetry of Earth's Atmosphere*. North Mankato, MN: Capstone, 2025.

Stroud, Jackie. *Under Your Feet: Soil, Sand, and Everything Underground*. New York: DK Publishing, 2020.

Turner, Myra Faye. *Unsolved Questions About Earth*. North Mankato, MN: Capstone, 2023.

SELECT BIBLIOGRAPHY OF AUTHOR'S RESEARCH

Barnes-Svarney, Patricia, and Thomas E. Svarney. *The Handy Geology Answer Book*. Detroit, MI: Visible Ink Press, 1999.

Robertson, Eugene C. "The Interior of the Earth." USGS, 2011. pubs.usgs.gov/gip/interior/

USGS. "How Does the Earth's Core Generate a Magnetic Field? | U.S. Geological Survey," December 16, 2013. usgs.gov/faqs/how-does-earths-core-generate-a-magnetic-field

Williams, Linda. *Earth Science Demystified*. Chicago: McGraw-Hill Education, 2004.

ABOUT THE AUTHOR

Kate Allen Fox is an award-winning children's author from southern California. After working in public health, she combined her passions for science and the written word and began writing picture books that inspire wonder and curiosity about the natural world, including: *Pando: A Living Wonder of Trees* (Capstone, 2021), which was named a Best Book of 2021 by *School Library Journal* and the Chicago Public Library, and was a finalist for the SCBWI Crystal Kite Award; *A Few Beautiful Minutes* (Little, Brown, 2023); and *Solstice Wish* (Beaming Books, 2024). Her essays have appeared in several publications, including *The New York Times* and *McSweeney's*. In addition to being a writer, Kate is a speaker, arts educator, and homeschooler. Find her online at kateallenfox.com.

ABOUT THE ILLUSTRATOR

Erin Brown is a Belfast-born Northern Irish illustrator who lives and works on the beautiful island of Jersey in the Channel Islands. After graduating university with a bachelors degree in Fine Art, she discovered a passion for stories and children's books. She combines her love for hand-drawn lines and traditional techniques with the flexibility and freedom of adding color digitally. When she's not working in her tiny studio, she can be found baking something overly sweet, exploring the forests and cliff paths of Jersey, or down at the seashore, watching the tide roll in.

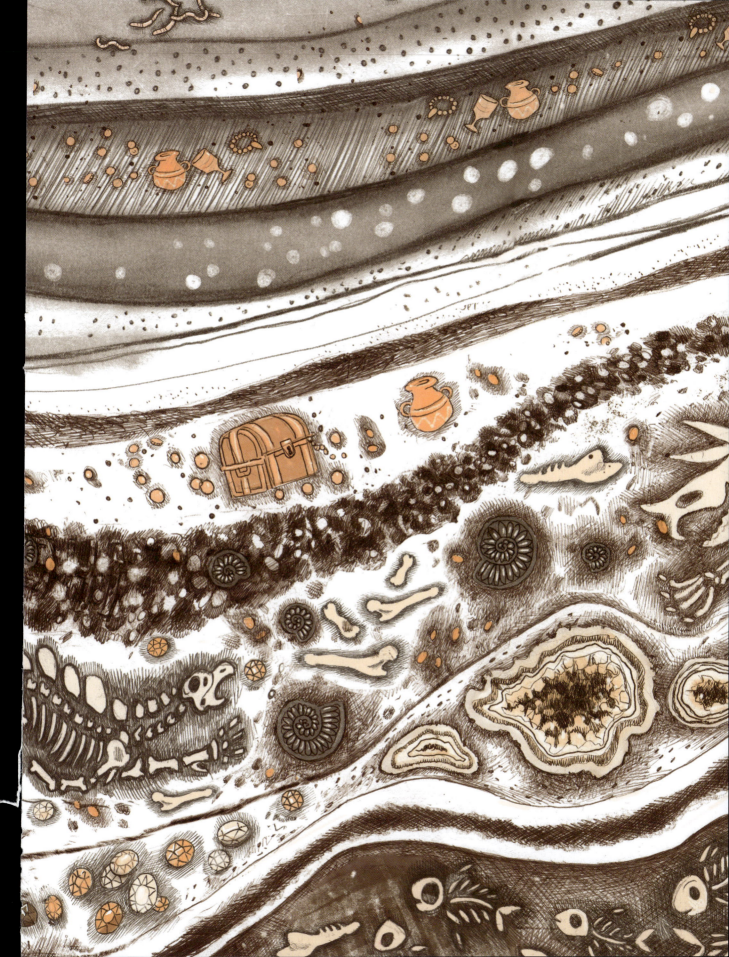